# First World War
## and Army of Occupation
# War Diary
## France, Belgium and Germany

28 DIVISION
84 Infantry Brigade
Monmouthshire Regiment (Territorial Force)
1st Battalion
13 February 1915 - 31 August 1915

WO95/2277/1

The Naval & Military Press Ltd
www.nmarchive.com
Published in association with The National Archives

Published by

## The Naval & Military Press Ltd

Unit 10 Ridgewood Industrial Park,

Uckfield, East Sussex,

TN22 5QE England

Tel: +44 (0) 1825 749494

www.naval-military-press.com

www.nmarchive.com

*This diary has been reprinted in facsimile from the original. Any imperfections are inevitably reproduced and the quality may fall short of modern type and cartographic standards.*

© **Crown Copyright**
**Images reproduced by permission of The National Archives, London, England, 2015.**

# Contents

| Document type | Place/Title | Date From | Date To |
|---|---|---|---|
| Heading | WO95/2277 1915 Feb-Aug 1 Battalion Monmouthshire Regiment Missing With Department. | | |
| Heading | ##################################################### | | |
| War Diary | Cambridge | 13/02/1915 | 14/02/1915 |
| War Diary | Havre | 15/02/1915 | 16/02/1915 |
| War Diary | Ryveld | 17/02/1915 | 26/02/1915 |
| War Diary | Dranoutre | 27/02/1915 | 28/02/1915 |
| War Diary | Havre to Cassel | | |
| War Diary | Clothing | | |
| Heading | 5th Division. 84th Brigade. The 84th Bde went to 5th Div from 28th Division on 22nd February, returning to 28th Div. 6th April 1915. War Diary 1st Monmouthshire Regiment March 1915 | | |
| War Diary | Dranoutre | 01/03/1915 | 07/03/1915 |
| War Diary | Wulverghem. | 08/03/1915 | 12/03/1915 |
| War Diary | Ravetsberg. | 13/03/1915 | 13/03/1915 |
| War Diary | Bailleul | 14/03/1915 | 16/03/1915 |
| War Diary | Ravetsberg. | 17/03/1915 | 18/03/1915 |
| War Diary | Dranoutre. | 19/03/1915 | 31/03/1915 |
| Heading | 28th Division. 84th Brigade. 7th 84th Bde Joined 28th Division 6/4/15 War Diary 1st Monmouthshire Regiment April 1915 | | |
| War Diary | Dranoutre | 31/03/1915 | 30/04/1915 |
| War Diary | Dranoutre | 01/04/1915 | 01/04/1915 |
| War Diary | Near Linpenhoek | 02/04/1915 | 05/04/1915 |
| War Diary | Reninghelst. | 06/04/1915 | 13/04/1915 |
| War Diary | Poperinge-Vlamertinghe | 13/04/1915 | 13/04/1915 |
| Operation(al) Order(s) | 84th Inf Bde Operation Order No. 19 App I | 03/04/1915 | 03/04/1915 |
| Miscellaneous | C Form (Quadruplicate). Messages And Signals. App II | | |
| Miscellaneous | C Form (Duplicate). Messages And Signals. App II | 04/04/1915 | 04/04/1915 |
| Miscellaneous | C Form (Quadruplicate). Messages And Signals. App III | | |
| Miscellaneous | A Form. Messages And Signals. App IV | | |
| Miscellaneous | B.M. 415. 1st Monmouth Regt. App V | 06/04/1915 | 06/04/1915 |
| Heading | 28th Division. 84th Brigade. War Diary 1st Monmouthshire Regiment 3rd to 15th & 28th to 31st May 1915 The Battalion was amalgamated with the 2nd & 3rd Monmouths on 28th May. | | |
| War Diary | | 01/05/1915 | 15/05/1915 |
| War Diary | | 03/05/1915 | 31/05/1915 |
| War Diary | Herzeele | 28/05/1915 | 31/05/1915 |
| Map | | | |
| Heading | 28th Division. 84th Brigade. War Diary Amalgamated Battalion of 1st, 2nd & 3rd Monmouthshires June 1915 | | |
| War Diary | Herzeele | 01/06/1915 | 11/06/1915 |
| War Diary | Rosenhillbek Reninghelst. | 12/06/1915 | 12/06/1915 |
| War Diary | Vierstraat | 13/06/1915 | 31/07/1915 |
| War Diary | Vierstraat | 01/07/1915 | 31/07/1915 |

| | | | |
|---|---|---|---|
| Heading | 28th Division 84th Brigade War Diary Amalgamated Battalion of 1st & 2nd Monmouthshires August 1915 Battalions resumed independant formation of August 11th 1915. 3rd Mons. Joined 83rd Bde. | | |
| War Diary | Lindenhoek | 01/08/1915 | 12/08/1915 |
| War Diary | Locre | 16/08/1915 | 20/08/1915 |
| War Diary | Lindenhoek | 13/08/1915 | 15/08/1915 |
| War Diary | Locre | 21/08/1915 | 31/08/1915 |
| Heading | WO95/Stray/YYY | | |

# PUBLIC RECORD OFFICE

Group/Class  WO 95
Piece  2277

1915 FEB - AUG

1 BATTALION MONMOUTHSHIRE
        REGIMENT

MISSING WITH DEPARTMENT

(date)
(Signed)

5th DIVISION.
84th Brigade.

The 84th Bde went to 5th Div from
28th Division on 22nd February,
returning to 28th Div. 6th April 1915.

# WAR DIARY

## 1st MONMOUTHSHIRE REGIMENT

### 13th to 28th FEBRUARY.

### 1915

Battalion disembarked at HAVRE 15.2.15.
Joined 84th Brigade 27.2.15.

Army Form C. 2118.

# WAR DIARY
## or
## INTELLIGENCE SUMMARY

(Erase heading not required.)

Instructions regarding War Diaries and Intelligence Summaries are contained in F.S. Regs., Part II. and the Staff Manual respectively. Title pages will be prepared in manuscript.

| Hour, Date, Place | Summary of Events and Information | Remarks and references to Appendices |
|---|---|---|
| Feb 13/1915. Cambridge | Battalion strength all ranks 1006. Left in 3 trains for Shaft. Entrained on SS CHYBASSA and SS CALEDONIAN. | Telegram received from GOC wires Division complimenting on good entrainment. E.D. |
| Feb 14th | Sailed from SOUTHAMPTON at 6 PM. | |
| Feb 15th HAVRE | Disembarked marched to REST CAMP. Completed equipment. | |
| Feb 16th HAVRE | Inspected by OC Rest camp. Completed equipment. Paraded to entrain at 10.30 am. Train left 4.00 pm. Ten platoons under Capt on Williams arrived at Rust. | E.D. APPEND I |
| Feb 17th RYVELD | Arrived CASSEL STATION 3.30 pm and got into billets at RYVELD by church. | journey & kit & carry E.D. |
| Feb 18th RYVELD | Changed billets. Capt on Williams and 2 platoons rejoined. | |
| Feb 19th & 21st | Route marching and steady work to get the men fit | E.D. |
| Feb 22nd — " — | also ordinary duties by night. Sir Horace Smith inspected the Battalion at work on experience. Satisfied with Battalion which was advancing in rapidly into which are my translators in into entrenching site and their general attitude. | E.D. NOTE |
| Feb 23rd — " — | Route march. E.D. | having to large regt of inf. and the Band large number |
| Feb 24th — " — | Entrenching by night E.D. | of men retiring from 2000 feet. |
| Feb 25th & 26th — " — | Route march | |
| Feb 27th DRANOUTRE | Battalion moved 9.30 am by Busses to FLETTRE thence by route march to DRANOUTRE. Journey to 84th Brigade. | |
| Feb 28th — " — | Whole day cleaning up billets which were very bad. | |

## APPENDIX I

**HAVRE to CASSEL**

The Train left HAVRE at 4-30 p.m. and did not arrive at CASSEL till 3.30 p.m. a journey of nearly 24 hours. During the whole of this time there was no halt of sufficient duration to allow of the men to make use of the latrines. There was one halt for watering horses only of 10 minutes duration, barely sufficient to give each horse a mouthful.

Proper halts for a fixed time are absolutely necessary. If a fixed halt can not be arranged beforehand The OC train should be informed at once of the probable duration of any halts on the way.

---

**Clothing.**

The Men at HAVRE were issued with large quantities of additional shirts and socks and FUR COATS this makes to big a load for a man to carry and additional Transport should be provided.

---

5th Division.
84th Brigade.

The 84th Bde went to 5th Div from
28th Division on 22nd February,
returning to 28th Div. 6th April 1915.

WAR DIARY

1st MONMOUTHSHIRE REGIMENT

*March*

1915

**WAR DIARY** or **INTELLIGENCE SUMMARY**

Army Form C. 2118.

*(Erase heading not required.)*

Instructions regarding War Diaries and Intelligence Summaries are contained in F. S. Regs, Part II. and the Staff Manual respectively. Title pages will be prepared in manuscript.

| Hour, Date, Place | Summary of Events and Information | Remarks and references to Appendices |
|---|---|---|
| March 1st 1915. DRANOUTRE | 10 Officers and 16 NCOs sent into the trenches for 24 hrs. | |
| 8 pm to 12 midnight | Working party 300 men from C & D Coys on fire and communication trenches. Fired on some of that kind. | |
| 2nd " | 1 Casualty slightly wounded in the head. E9. | |
| | 8 Officers and 16 NCOs into trenches for 24 hours | |
| 3rd " | C & D Coys provided working parts in trenches. E9. | |
| | Company parades. Turning out & kit inspection at C.B. | |
| 4th " | D Company in trenches with QVR 9th London. | |
| | 3 Platoons C Coy digging fatigue. E9 | |
| 5th " | A & B Coy in Trenches with 9th QVR. E9 | |
| 6th " | C Coy in trenches with 9 QVR Rifles – Captain C.W. Hatton | |
| | to England to purchase running machinery – E9 | |
| 7th " | 1 Company in trenches with 9th QVR Rifles – Dug out | |
| 8th " | } Two companies and Headquarters took over section | |
| 9th WULVERGHEM. | } of trenches from 9th QVR Rifles. Sent out patrols in B Coys | |
| | could discover no sign of any sapping. Improved | | / hour
| | trenches and started a file in front between 10A & 10B. | |
| 10th " | Two casualties 1 killed 1 wounded. C.B. out. | |
| | The Germans shelled WULVERGHEM but there was no one | |
| | in the village. 4 49cot | |
| 11th " | So fondant. Day normal. C.B. | |

Army Form C. 2118.

# WAR DIARY
## or
## INTELLIGENCE SUMMARY
*(Erase heading not required.)*

Instructions regarding War Diaries and Intelligence Summaries are contained in F. S. Regs., Part II. and the Staff Manual respectively. Title pages will be prepared in manuscript.

| Hour, Date, Place | Summary of Events and Information | Remarks and references to Appendices |
|---|---|---|
| 12/5 March 1915 | 8.30 a.m. Opened rapid fire to cover our attack. | |
| | 8.55 a.m. Received orders cancelling orders to keep enemy to division on telephone wires. | |
| | 9.30 a.m. A large quantity of ammunition being expended on 10A trench. Lieut Stewart with 6 bats was sent up with 19 boxes S.A.A. He carried 104 without rest by details along N side of MESSINES road. | |
| | 4 p.m. Fire of gun opened at rate of 5 rounds per minute on enfilade gun fire at direction. | |
| | 5.45 p.m. | |
| | 7.15 p.m. Relieved by 3rd Arm. Regt. Marched to RAVETSBERG. One gun was but ... L.Co Coy [?] (en route) | 1 man |
| 13/5 RAVETSBERG | Rested. | |
| 14/5 BAILLEUL | Marched to BAILLEUL and took over billets of 2nd Cheshires. Lt.D.Colt. | |
| 15/5 " | Rested. Receiving orders & arms & PLOEGSTREET when our casualties left. | |
| 16/5 " | Rested and rebel. L.D.Colt. | |
| 17/5 RAVETSBERG | Marched to RAVETSBERG and took over billets 3rd Arm Regt. Battalion Route march. Lt.D.Colt. | |
| 18/5 " | | |
| 19/5 DRANOUTRE | Moved into billets at RAVETSBERG DRANOUTRE | |
| 20/5 " | Battalion in Reserve. 118 | |
| 21/5 " | Working party 200 men in Trenches | |
| 22nd " | Working party 200 men in Trenches casualties 2 killed 2 wounded. L.D. | |

Army Form C. 2118.

# WAR DIARY
## or
## INTELLIGENCE SUMMARY.
(Erase heading not required.)

| Place | Date | Hour | Summary of Events and Information | Remarks and references to |
|---|---|---|---|---|
| DRANOUTRE | 23rd March 1915 | | Drills and cleaning up. EO. | |
| " | 24 | 5.45 p.m. | A Coy (Capt CARRICK) to duty in trenches with Suffolk Regt. | |
| " | " | 6 pm | B Coy (Capt LC Llewelin) D Coy (Capt HT Edwards) to duty in the trenches with Welsh Regt. | |
| " | 25 | 6 pm | C Coy found working parties to Welsh Regt. | |
| " | 26 | " | C Coy found working parties to Welsh Regt. | |
| " | 27 | " | A. B. D companies in trenches A Coy attached SUFFOLKS B & D Coys attached WELCH REGT | |
| " | 28 | " | ditto received EO. | 1 man |
| " | 29 | " | ditto Battalion rested in trenches at DRANOUTRE LeOCafé | |
| " | 31 | " | ditto - LB | |
| " | 31st | | A & B Coys. working parties on trenches - C, D Coys Rest | |

28th Division.
84th Brigade.

The 84th Bde rejoined 28th Division 6/4/15

WAR DIARY

1st MONMOUTHSHIRE REGIMENT

April

1 9 1 5

Army Form C. 2118.

# WAR DIARY
## or
## INTELLIGENCE SUMMARY.
(Erase heading not required.)

Instructions regarding War Diaries and Intelligence Summaries are contained in F.S.Regs., Part II and the Staff Manual respectively. Title pages will be prepared in manuscript.

| Hour, Date, Place | Summary of Events and Information | Remarks and references to Appendices |
|---|---|---|
| March 31st 1915 DRANOUTRE | A & B Coys working parties on trenches C & D Coys Rest. | |
| April 1st 1915 DRANOUTRE | Took over centre sector of trenches held by 84th Brigade. Relief carried out with no casualties. – C & D in fire trenches. | |
| April 2nd 1915 DRANOUTRE | In trenches. 11a.m. Germans shelling in direction of SPY FARM. 1 Rfn wounded | |
| April 3rd 1915 DRANOUTRE | C & D Coys relieved by A & B Companies. CO & Adjt. 2nd in Command & Officers 4th Leicesters came to inspect trenches. 3 Rfn wounded. Lt Wilson and 2Lt Newland, Edwards James & Williams joined the Battalion from England. | |

Army Form C. 2118.

# WAR DIARY
## or
## INTELLIGENCE SUMMARY.
*(Erase heading not required.)*

Instructions regarding War Diaries and Intelligence Summaries are contained in F.S. Regs., Part II. and the Staff Manual respectively. Title pages will be prepared in manuscript.

| Hour, Date, Place | Summary of Events and Information | Remarks and references to Appendices |
|---|---|---|
| April 4th 1915 | 5-15 Germans shelled GABLE FARM setting it on fire. Battalion relieved by 4th Leicesters Regiment and marched to billets in DRANOUTRE. Relief completed 3-40 a.m. | |
| April 5th 1915 | Battalion marched from DRANOUTRE to RENINGHELST and joined 14th Brigade. | |
| April 6th 1915 | Rested. Battalion reverted to 81st Brigade. | |
| April 7th 1915 | Battalion marched into LOCRE for inspection with 84th Brigade by General Sir Horace Smith Dorrien. | |
| April 8th 9th 10th | In billets at RENINGHELST. | |

# WAR DIARY
## or
## INTELLIGENCE SUMMARY.

*(Erase heading not required.)*

Army Form C. 2118.

Instructions regarding War Diaries and Intelligence Summaries are contained in F.S. Regs., Part II and the Staff Manual respectively. Title pages will be prepared in manuscript.

| Hour, Date, Place | Summary of Events and Information | Remarks and references to Appendices |
|---|---|---|
| April 11th 1915 | Battalion marched into LOCRE for Inspection by Sir J. French | |
| April 12th 1915 | In billets at RENINGHELST | |
| April 13th 1915 | Marched at 10a.m. via POPERINGHE to billets on the POPERINGHE – VLAMERTINGHE road | |
| April 14th 1915 | In Billets on POPERINGHE – VLAMERTINGHE Road. Arranged to entertain a CANADIAN Battn. which however passed straight through to Ypres. | |
| April 15th 1915 | In Billets. Route Marching by Companies. Drove experimental bore hole & fired mine successfully. 4.30p.m. received orders to stand by | |

# WAR DIARY
## or
## INTELLIGENCE SUMMARY.
*(Erase heading not required.)*

Army Form C. 2118.

| Hour, Date, Place | Summary of Events and Information | Remarks and references to Appendices |
|---|---|---|
| April 16th 1915. | Marched at 1-0 p.m. (via VLAMERTINGHE) to YPRES. Billeted in ECOLE COMMUNALE (O.O. Order 21) "B" Coy advanced to Billets in farm near FREZENBERG (BM.6.4.) | |
| April 17th 1915. | "A" "C" "D" Coys in billets at YPRES. Physical drill &c. "B" Co. detailed to repair fire trenches at BROODSEINDE Crossroads at night. Unable to work owing to activity of German trench mortars & Stretcher bearers did good work. Heavy bombardment of trenches S.E. of YPRES (HILL 60) in conjunction with the blowing up of German trenches by mines in the construction of which a detachment of the Battn. had taken a prominent part. Operations here very successful. | |

Army Form C. 2118.

# WAR DIARY
## or
## INTELLIGENCE SUMMARY.
(Erase heading not required.)

Instructions regarding War Diaries and Intelligence Summaries are contained in F. S. Regs., Part II. and the Staff Manual respectively. Title pages will be prepared in manuscript.

| Hour, Date, Place | Summary of Events and Information | Remarks and references to Appendices |
|---|---|---|
| April 18th 1915. | "A" & "C" Coys marched at 6.50 a.m. to farm at FREZENBERG. In reserve. "B" Coy returned to YPRES. No. 2 Platoon shelled on the road of FREZENBERG. One casualty — slightly wounded in neck. | |
| April 19th 1915. | "A" & "C" Coys on digging fatigue in trenches on night 18/19th. Two casualties — 2 R.h. wounded (by bomb). "B" & "D" Coys in Billets at YPRES. Town shelled in morning and afternoon, several casualties (outside He. Batty.) Seven Officers proceeded to trenches at night (Nos 17 & 20) to view positions, preparatory to taking over from 12th London French D'Orleans (Divisions) under Lieut Cottrill "E" Coy. Successful in silencing German Minenwerfer in Suffolk trenches. "A" & "C" Company engaged in digging fire trenches covering head at BROODSEINDE cross roads. | BROODSEINDE CROSSROADS BIRDCAGE New F.T. |

Army Form C. 2118.

# WAR DIARY
## or
## INTELLIGENCE SUMMARY.
*(Erase heading not required.)*

Instructions regarding War Diaries and Intelligence Summaries are contained in F.S. Regs., Part II and the Staff Manual respectively. Title pages will be prepared in manuscript.

| Hour, Date, Place | Summary of Events and Information | Remarks and references to Appendices |
|---|---|---|
| April 20th 1915 | "A" Co returned from digging fatigue to YPRES at 4/30 am — Casualties 3 wounded Lt Cottrell in trenches with last section Trench Mortar Casualties 1 wounded YPRES heavily shelled in late morning & afternoon. One shell proved to be from a 17" gun Casualties among troops reinforcing numerous Casualties (on the Battn.) 2 wounded Lt Jumper to trenches at night to reiew (?) in coming out his guide was wounded Total Casualties 7 wounded | |

Army Form C. 2118.

# WAR DIARY
## or
## INTELLIGENCE SUMMARY.
*(Erase heading not required.)*

Instructions regarding War Diaries and Intelligence Summaries are contained in F.S. Regs., Part II. and the Staff Manual respectively. Title pages will be prepared in manuscript.

| Hour, Date, Place | Summary of Events and Information | Remarks and references to Appendices |
|---|---|---|
| April 21st 1915. | In consequence of the heavy shelling during the preceding days all troops were sent out of YPRES. The Battalion marched out by Companies at 7.30 a.m. to fields W. of ST JEAN. In the afternoon orders were received cancelling the intended relief of 12th London trenches. The Battalion accordingly bivouacked the hedges & in shelter trenches which they dug. Lt Cottrell in trenches with Essex Divl. Cavalry — Nil | |
| April 22nd 1915. | 3pm. Battalion moved by companies to VELORENHOEK being met there by 1st LINE transport. Operation orders No 23 were cancelled and orders issued for relief of 12th London which were subsequently cancelled. Battalion bivouaced under hedges for the night. Battalion Rations handed over to 12th London and own rations not received till 12 noon 23rd. Battalion in bivouac at VELORENHOEK. Heavy shelling to the N of Salient and eyes smart strongly | |

# WAR DIARY
## or
## INTELLIGENCE SUMMARY.

Army Form C. 2118.

| Hour, Date, Place | Summary of Events and Information | Remarks and references to Appendices |
|---|---|---|
| April 23rd 1915 | Day spent in Bivouac at VERLORENHOEK. Relieved 12th London Regt. in trenches Nd of ZONNEBEKE. No. 20 - 18 - 19. B + D in trenches C + A in supports. Rations: 2 Lt Stealey reported for duty and was posted to "C" Company. Transport was shelled on the road through MENINGATE. Casualties: Sgt. J. Morgan, Transport Sgt. killed. Q.M.S. Shuttle wounded. | |
| April 24th 1915 | B + D Coys. trenches A + C supports. 18 trench heavily bombarded with rifle grenades causing casualties. 2 Officers wounded 6 Other Ranks killed and 13 wounded. Very trying for men having no means of reply. A Company reinforced No 20 trench by 1 Platoon. This party was observed from a German balloon and was | |

# WAR DIARY
## or
## INTELLIGENCE SUMMARY.
(Erase heading not required.)

Army Form C. 2118.

| Hour, Date, Place | Summary of Events and Information | Remarks and references to Appendices |
|---|---|---|
| April 24th 1915 | Heavily shelled on the way up. Having 6 casualties. Situation generally quiet throughout the night. Casualties. Trench stores required Sandbags 3000 2 Stands for firing Rifle Grenades. Chevaux de frise. Considerable difficulty in obtaining stores and could only get 30 Rifle Grenades. Slight shelling during the day. C Coy (Capt. B.L. Percy) ordered out to report to Major BARRETT N.F. at ZONNEBEKE Church. | |

Army Form C. 2118.

# WAR DIARY
## or
## INTELLIGENCE SUMMARY.
*(Erase heading not required.)*

Instructions regarding War Diaries and Intelligence Summaries are contained in F. S. Regs., Part II. and the Staff Manual respectively. Title pages will be prepared in manuscript.

| Hour, Date, Place | Summary of Events and Information | Remarks and references to Appendices |
|---|---|---|
| April 25th 1915. | Work done during the night. Improvement of fire trenches and constructing traverses. These not having been considered necessary by the French. | |
| 11-15 a.m. | Trench 20 was heavily shelled from left front. Germans commenced an attack on trench 20 which was immediately repulsed with Rifle fire and Shrapnel. The Battery opening at exactly the right moment. Remainder of the day comparatively quiet but 18 trench still suffered from Rifle Grenades. C. Company still away. Unable to carry out relief only having 3 Platoons A Coy in support. Casualties. Work done. Improving trenches & communications. Building Dug outs in 18 trench to protect men from Rifle Grenades. Not sufficient grenades having been sent to make any effective reply. | |

# WAR DIARY
## or
## INTELLIGENCE SUMMARY.
(Erase heading not required.)

Army Form C. 2118.

| Hour, Date, Place | Summary of Events and Information | Remarks and references to Appendices |
|---|---|---|
| April 25th 1915 | 5 pm Tyne & Tees Brigade made an advance along N. of railway at ZONNEBEKE under very heavy artillery fire. They advanced very steadily as far as could be seen. | |
| April 26th 1915. | "C" Company returned at 12/20am. Reported by Capt. Birkett to Attached Limits. 30 Men H.Q.O.R. Capt. R.L. Perry killed. 5.30 am. Large number of men seen returning along railroad N. of ZONNEBEKE. Lt. Cottrell returned with M.G. Section. 1 Platoon of Coy was fetched up from the Ramparts. Major E.S. Williams stopped a good many men returning. 1 Shell in 20 trench wounded 2 Officers Coy Sgt Major & 3 other ranks "B" Co. 1 Killed 1 man. | |
| April 27th. 1915. | Situation quiet all day. Carried out small reliefs. (when falling in a shell burst among the draft killing wounding 3) Draft of 20 joined the Battalion. Lieut. Cottell with 1 trench mortar sent to No 18 French Casualties. | |

Army Form C. 2118.

# WAR DIARY
## or
## INTELLIGENCE SUMMARY.
*(Erase heading not required.)*

Instructions regarding War Diaries and Intelligence Summaries are contained in F. S. Regs., Part II. and the Staff Manual respectively. Title pages will be prepared in manuscript.

| Hour, Date, Place | Summary of Events and Information | Remarks and references to Appendices |
|---|---|---|
| April 28th 1915 | Situation quiet all day. Trench mortar in 18 trench most effective and entirely stopped Rifle Grenade fire. Small works carried out in trenches. | |
| April 29th 1915 | | |
| April 30th 1915 | Situation quiet no incident to report. Work was carried on as fast as possible improving, masking traverses in trenches also communication. | |

# WAR DIARY
## or
## INTELLIGENCE SUMMARY.

Army Form C. 2118.

| Place | Date | Hour | Summary of Events and Information | Remarks and references to Appendices |
|---|---|---|---|---|
| | April 1st | — | | |
| April 2nd over LINDENHOEK | | — | Battalion took over centre sector of trenches held by 84th Brigade. 1/4B 11am German shelled in direction of SPY FARM. 1 P/hr wounded. 1/4B | |
| April 3rd | | — | C & D Coys relieved by A & B. 1/4B C.O. adjt. 2nd in command and a officers 4th Leicester Regt. came to inspect trenches. 3 the Rfm. Wounded. L.J | |

**WAR DIARY**
or
**INTELLIGENCE SUMMARY**

*(Erase heading not required.)*

Army Form C. 2118.

| Hour, Date, Place | Summary of Events and Information | Remarks and references to Appendices |
|---|---|---|
| April 4th nr LINDENHOEK 5.15 pm | Germans shelled GABLE Fm setting it on fire. | |
| 10.30 pm | Commenced relief by 4th Bn LEICESTER REGT. LDCot | APP II |
| April 5th 3-45 am | Relief completed. | |
| 1 p.m. | Battalion marched out to billets at DRANOUTRE. | |
| | Battalion marched to Billets near RENINGHELSE. and joined 14th Brigade. | APP III IV |
| April 6th RENINGHELSE. | Battalion reverted LDCot | |
| 3 pm | Battalion reverted to 8th Brigade. LDCot | APP V |
| April 7th RENINGHELSE. 2.30 pm | Battalion marched into LOCRE for inspection by General Sir Horace Smith-Dorrien. LDCot | |
| April 8th 9th RENINGHELSE 10th | in billets | |
| April 11th RENINGHELSE | Battalion marched into LOCRE for inspection and Reviewed by General Sir H PLUMER. LDCot in billets | |
| April 12th RENINGHELSE | in billets | |
| April 13th POPERINGE - VLAMERTINGHE 10 am | Marched from RENINGHELSE via POPERINGE & billets on the POPERINGHE - VLAMERTINGHE Road LDCot | |

app I

Copy No. ........

## 84th Inf Bde Operation Order No.19.

Reference 1/10000 Sketch Map.

Headquarters,
3rd April.1915.

1. Trench Batons of the 84th Inf Bde will be relieved by Batons of the North Mid Div, on the 4th/5th ~~~~~~~~ April.

2. (a) 1st Suff R, less 1 Officer and 25 men in F.2 and M.Gun in S.P.2b, will be relieved by 7th Notts & Derby R (Notts & Derby Bde) on the 4th/5th April.

(b) Relieve Companies 1st Suff R, will be South of LINDENHOEK CROSS ROADS by 11-30.p.m. and will not pass LINDENHOEK GUARD until 12m.n.

(c) 7th Notts & Derby R from HEMMEL, is due at LINDENHOEK CROSS ROADS 11-30.p.m. 4th, and will be met there by two guides 1st Suff R for each trench, viz. F.2, F.4, F.5, F.6 and S.P.3.
The reliefs will start from these Cross Roads at 12m.n.

(d) O.C.1st Suff R will remain in command of his sector until the relief is completed.

(e) After relief 1st Suff R will return to billets in DRANOUTRE ~~lately occupied by the 1st Mon'th R.~~ (Minden & Dettigen Huts)

3. (a) 1st Welch R less garrison of E.1 trench but ~~~~ plus garrison 1st Mon'th in E.4, will be relieved by 5th Leic R (Lincoln & Leicester Bde) on 4th/5th April.

(b) 5th Leic R from DRANOUTRE is due at PACKHORSE FARM 11-30p.m. and will be met there by two guides 1st Welch R for each of following trenches, viz, 14, 14S, 15, 15S, E.4 and S.P.1: the reliefs will start from PACKHORSE FARM at 12m.n.

(c) O.C.1st Welch R will remain in command of his sector until the relief is completed.

(d) After relief 1st Welch R will return to LOURE HUTS evacuated by 5th Leic R, and the 1st Mon'th garrison of E.4 will go into its Batn Reserve.

4. (a) 1st Mon'th R with Suff Detachment in F.2, Suff M.Gun in S.P.2b and Welch garrison in E.1 will be relieved by 4th Leic R on 5th/6th April.

(b) 4th Leic R is due from DRANOUTRE at ONTREL FARM ~~11-30p.m.~~ 10.pm and will be met there by two guides 1st Mon'th R for each of following trenches, viz, E.1, E.2, E.3, E.6, F.2, S.P.2a and S.P.2b: two guides 1st Welch R for E.1 will meet the relief on arrival at E.3: reliefs will start from ONTREL FARM at ~~12m.n.~~ 10.30p.m.

(c) O.C.1st Mon'th R will remain in command of his sector until the relief is completed.

(d) After relief 1st Monmouth R will return to DRANOUTRE.

~~5~~ 6. Reports as at present.

5. ~~Ches R~~ will move to BAILLEUL afternoon 4th inst

Issued at.........

H.Walford Major.
Brigade Major.
84th Infantry Brigade.

App II

"C" Form (Quadruplicate).      Army Form C. 2123 A.
MESSAGES AND SIGNALS.      No. of Message...............

| | Charges to Pay £  s.  d. | Office Stamp. |

Service Instructions.

Handed in at the..............Office, at............m. Received here at............m

TO     (Con tnd)

| Sender's Number | Day of Month | In reply to Number. | AAA |
|---|---|---|---|
| Para | 4 B | for | 11 30 |
| pm | Substitute | 10.0 | pm |
| and | for | 12 | M |
| M. | Substitute | 10 30 | pm |
| aaa | acknowledge | | |

FROM   84th Brigade
PLACE
TIME   9.56 am

GALE & POLDEN, LTD. PRINTERS, ALDERSHOT.
(69,017). Wt. 7081—413. 40,000 Pads. 4/18. W.

App II

"C" Form (Duplicate).    Army Form C. 2123 A.
MESSAGES AND SIGNALS.    No. of Message..........

APP II | Charges to Pay £ s. d. | Office Stamp. ZHD 4/4/15

Service Instructions.

Handed in at the 3 HD Office, at 9.55 m. Received here at ....... m.

TO: 1st Monmouth Regt

| Sender's Number | Day of Month. | In reply to Number. | AAA |
|---|---|---|---|
| BM 341 | 4th | | |
| Reference | operation | order | number |
| 19 | aaa | all | our |
| 3 | section | will | be |
| relieved | tonight | aaa | following |
| amendments | | will | be |
| made | in | O | P |
| order | 19 | aaa | Para |
| 1 | delete | and | ~~~~ |
| 5th/6 | aaa | Para | 2 |
| C | delete | 3 | 2 |
| aaa | Para | 4 | a |
| for | 5th/6 | | april |
| substitute | 4th/5 | april | aaa |

FROM
PLACE
TIME

App III

"C" Form (Quadruplicate).     Army Form C. 2123 A.

## MESSAGES AND SIGNALS.

APP III

Handed in at the 7th D Office at 6.15 p.m. Received here at 6.30 p.m.

TO 1st Mon R

| Sender's Number | Day of Month | In reply to Number | AAA |
|---|---|---|---|
| Bm 369 | 7.2 | | |
| You | will | march | tomorrow |
| at | 1.0 p.m | Sta | LOCRE |
| and | ZEVECOTEN | | to |
| BICEPS | near | RENINGHELSE | |
| and | on | arrival | there |
| come | under | orders | of |
| 14th | Inf | Bde | forming |
| part | of | that | Brigade |
| aaa | your | billeting | party |
| will | report | to | Staff |
| Captain | 83rd | Bde | at |
| Westoutre | at | 11.0 a.m | tomorrow |
| aaa | acknowledge | | |

FROM 84th Brigade
PLACE
TIME 6.15 p.m.

App IV

## "A" Form.
### MESSAGES AND SIGNALS.
Army Form C. 2121.

App IV

| Sender's Number | Day of Month | In reply to Number | AAA |
|---|---|---|---|
| B.M 870 | 4" | | |

Operation Order No 173 AAA Reference Map 1/40,000 AAA Troops to move from LOCRE and vicinity tomorrow as follows AAA Devons to pass road junction in M.17.c at 9-45.A.M. and march via LA CLYTTE to billets in huts just north of road in H.32.a AAA Cheshires to pass road junction in M.17.c at 10 AM and march via LA CLYTTE to billets in huts south of road in H.32.a AAA O/Surreys to pass road junction in M.17.c at 10-15.AM and march via LA CLYTTE to huts south of road in M.6.a AAA Train to pass road junction in M.17.c at 10-30.AM. and march via WESTOUTRE and RENINGHELST to billets in G.35.c AAA 14th Field Ambulance to pass road junction in M.17.c at 10-45 AM and march by WESTOUTRE and RENINGHELST to billets in OUDERDOM AAA Billeting parties to meet Staff Captain at LA CLYTTE cross roads at 9AM. AAA 1st Monmouths will move into billets in neighbourhood of RENINGHELST tomorrow and on reaching that place

## "A" Form.
## MESSAGES AND SIGNALS.

Army Form C. 2121.

*(form fields, blank)*

(2)   AAA

will come under orders of Brigadier General Commanding and form part of Brigade AAA Units are warned that water in or about OOSTERDOM is not too good and Medical Officers should take steps to test same and in any case boiling should be resorted to AAA Bde Hd Qrs will remain at LOCRE till further orders AAA Acknowledge.

From 14th Inf Bde
Place
Time 8.55 PM

W Dick Cunyngham Major

APP V

B.M.415.

1st Monmouth Regt.

"First Monmouth now billeted North of RENINGHELST reverts to 84th Brigade on receipt of this wire AAA Acknowledge AAA Addressed 14th and 84th Infantry Bde."

(No. G.965 from 5th Div)

The above message is/forwarded for your information.

Brigade Headquarters is in St JANS CAPPEL.

Please send two cycle dispatch riders to Brigade Head Quarters at once. They will be rationed by us.

Also please inform me where your Head Qtrs and Billets are situated.

Walford
Major.
Headquarters.                          Brigade Major.
6th April 1915.                        84th Infantry Brigade.

28th Division.
84th Brigade.

WAR DIARY

1st MONMOUTHSHIRE REGIMENT

~~2nd to 15th & 28th to 31st~~

MAY

1915

The Battalion was amalgamated with the 2nd & 3rd Monmouths on 28th May.

Army Form C. 2118.

# WAR DIARY
## or
## INTELLIGENCE SUMMARY.
*(Erase heading not required.)*

Instructions regarding War Diaries and Intelligence Summaries are contained in F. S. Regs., Part II. and the Staff Manual respectively. Title pages will be prepared in manuscript.

| Place | Date | Hour | Summary of Events and Information | Remarks and references to Appendices |
|---|---|---|---|---|
| | May 1st, 1915. | | Situation quiet. Headquarters shelled slightly during the day. Wounded from dressing station moved into the cellars. Casualties — | |
| | May 2nd 1915 | | Situation quiet. Further shelling of Hd Qrs. Casualties — | |
| | May 3 – 15th, 1915. Exclusive | | Records missing – x | |

x Diary from 3rd May continued on next page.

# WAR DIARY or INTELLIGENCE SUMMARY

Army Form C. 2118.

| Hour, Date, Place | Summary of Events and Information | Remarks and references to Appendices |
|---|---|---|
| May 3rd 1915 | The 2 Companies in the firing line were A & D and 1 Platoon of C. D. Coy held Trench 18 under Capt Hy Edwards & part of B Coy held trenches 19a. 19b, 19c & 20. B. Co in ZONNEBEKE Brickworks & remainder of C. Co in dug outs near level crossing. Trenches 19a, 19b, 19c & 20 were only joined up by very bad communication trenches & great care had to be taken in passing between them in daylight. These trenches were on the South side of the Cross Roads at BROODSEINDE (see sketch appended). Trench No 21 was held on this date by the 2/Northumberland Fusiliers, (under Command of the late Capt WREFORD-BROWN, D.S.O (killed in action 24 May 1915) Trench 21 was within 12 yards of the enemy & a portion of it was | + |

# WAR DIARY
## or
## INTELLIGENCE SUMMARY
(Erase heading not required.)

Army Form C. 2118.

| Hour, Date, Place | Summary of Events and Information | Remarks and references to Appendices |
|---|---|---|
| May 3rd/1915 contd | known as the International trench - having been occupied by french Germans & British close to this trench there was a small fortified work known as the BIRD CAGE occupied by Germans, having wire over the top as protection against Bombs. At midday orders were received for all Company Commanders to meet C.O. at Battn Hdqrs at 3 p.m. This meeting was held in the cellar of the Convent at ZONNEBEKE. Lt. Col. Robinson informed them that orders had been received for a general retirement from the salient to a position in rear of FREZENBERG. Instructions to Company Commanders were as follows:- First. These Companies in Support were to move responding at Railway Level Crossing West of | |

Army Form C. 2118.

# WAR DIARY
## or
## INTELLIGENCE SUMMARY
(Erase heading not required.)

| Hour, Date, Place | Summary of Events and Information | Remarks and references to Appendices |
|---|---|---|
| May 3rd 1915 contd. | ZONNEBEKE to Staff Officers & companies in the fire trenches were to withdraw at 10-30 p.m. having previously sent back surplus ammunition. Parties of 1 Officer & 30 men per Co. were to be left in trenches to continue firing & sending up very lights. These parties were commanded by 2/Lt B.T. VACHELL & 2/Lt E.S. PHILLIPS & were not to leave until midnight. & companies were to be withdrawn quietly & taken to Staff Officers by 11 o'clock p.m. & were not to leave the level crossing until midnight. Nothing of use to the enemy was to be left behind. By any bombay. What could not be taken out was burned or otherwise disposed of. B. Co. in ZONNEBEKE Brickworks put into the well there, several boxes of ammunition & also several sacks of bully beef. The movement was carried out quite successfully without casualties, the whole | |

# WAR DIARY or INTELLIGENCE SUMMARY

Army Form C. 2118.

| Hour, Date, Place | Summary of Events and Information | Remarks and references to Appendices |
|---|---|---|
| May 3rd/1915 contd. | Regiment marched to Hutts near BRIELEN North of YPRES. Preparing to Brigade as they passed VERLORENHOEK. The whole of the 28th Division retired at dawn. The road ZONNEBEKE–YPRES. There was no shelling of the road until near the MENIN GATE & it was unnecessary to leave the road. The road itself was pitted with shell holes & the bombardment of the preceding days. Dead horses & broken down Ambulances were passed en route to YPRES, dead civilians. The parties left in trenches left at midnight after taking their way independently reached the Huts safely. The following incidents are worthy of record. (1) The same Communication trench served fire trenches 19, 20 & 21. N.F's. the trench garrison of 19 & 20 were withdrawn first. Major Ewill was warned by note that of the N.F's. & about 9–30 p.m. that a strange noise | |

Army Form C. 2118.

# WAR DIARY
or
## INTELLIGENCE SUMMARY

(Erase heading not required.)

Instructions regarding War Diaries and Intelligence Summaries are contained in F. S. Regs., Part II. and the Staff Manual respectively. Title pages will be prepared in manuscript.

| Hour, Date, Place | Summary of Events and Information | Remarks and references to Appendices |
|---|---|---|
| May 3rd 1915 contd. | Presumably German had tried to pass over the French front. The British side. He was found next to a officer in the darkness. The officer however was that the night easy have produced among both the German line over face communication from his Between 19 a 19 c & 19 c & 20. Major Ewell sent out a patrol to try to capture this man without avail. It is quite certain that the Germans had suspected this reconnaissance, the ZONNEBEKE PRES road would have been made impassable by shellfire & that there would have been divisible no loss of life. (2) About an hour after Lt. F. D. Phillips had been left with his party of 30 men in trench 18, a German flare was fired over his trench & set on fire the thatched roof of his fire behind his trench, illuminating the trench from behind. Young recover to think that German suspicions were aroused. He noted the time & had still half an hour to remain in French Sarriean, the time however passed without further event. | |

1247  W 3299  200,000 (E)  8/14  J.B.C. & A.    Forms/C. 2118/11.

Army Form C. 2118.

# WAR DIARY
## or
## INTELLIGENCE SUMMARY

*(Erase heading not required.)*

Instructions regarding War Diaries and Intelligence Summaries are contained in F.S. Regs., Part II. and the Staff Manual respectively. Title pages will be prepared in manuscript.

| Hour, Date, Place | Summary of Events and Information | Remarks and references to Appendices |
|---|---|---|
| May 4th 1915. | Day spent at rest at Hudson near BRIELEN, YPRES. Draft arrived 40 N.C.O's & men. | |
| May 5th 1915. | Whole BRIELEN, owing to the enemy having moved to shorter their lines in field were getting into they they wanted the day time. YPRES remains roomy by itself. | |
| May 6th do | Bright fine day. In the afternoon Officers had foot races in field in rear of Hudson's House. Returns to beings Leading party about 4pm was met on bye at (unluckily came with orders to move at once by a reconnaissance identifying YPRES - to dig outs east of POTIJZE. E 29 c 23 (reference Map. Sheet 28 B.I. 1/40,000). These dig outs were nothing more than old incomplete trenches, very wet. 2 Coys were detailed to dig posts, one for 1/2 th London Regt. as we were coming to Trenches subsequently to be taken over by the Battn. next evening. Heavy howy. fire was opened by the enemy in early hours of morning May 1st |

Form/C. 2118/11.

# WAR DIARY or INTELLIGENCE SUMMARY

Army Form C. 2118.

(Erase heading not required.)

| Hour, Date, Place | Summary of Events and Information | Remarks and references to Appendices |
|---|---|---|
| August 19th 1915. | Both remained in the day outside which were severely shelled. 1st Bn. casualties — among them Lt.-Col. Brown. Cpt. 60 killed. At night Battn. marched to relieve 12th London Regt. see sketch attached which approximately shows the line of trench occupied by the Battn. Reference sheet 28bis 1. 40,000. The line runs from road 6.23.b.51 to road 6.30.d.55. 500 yards as to disposition of Companies. The trenches had been badly broken down in some parts demolished by the fire of previous days. The 12th London had suffered heavily by shell fire. Communication trenches to rear were very shallow in some cases full of water. Headquarters were close to the road chosen at a point about 6.23.d.58 (Map 28). The night was spent in repairing the trenches as far as was possible to do so in the few hours of darkness left. There was no protection again shell fire. The trench | B |

# WAR DIARY
## or
## INTELLIGENCE SUMMARY

*(Erase heading not required.)*

Army Form C. 2118

| Place | Date | Hour | Summary of Events and Information | Remarks and references to Appendices |
|---|---|---|---|---|
| | 1915 May 8 | | Strength of the regiment was Officers 23 & other ranks 565. The intense German bombardment, described afterwards by Sir John French when he addressed the Brigade at HERZEELE, as probably the heaviest to which the troops had ever been subjected, began at about 6.30 am. As the morning wore on there were many casualties in our trenches. A German Infantry attack was launched somewhere about the junction of the 84th & 83rd Brigades & the line was first broken south of the YPRES-ZONNEBEKE Road. Once the enemy Infantry had broken through the action became a flank as well as frontal attack, as far as our Brigade was concerned. A heavy machine gun fire from the left flank was directed without ceasing & the trench on the right of the section Heavily & gradually widened. Men of another regiment were seen & our men to fall back & wander on our right & shortly afterwards men of yet another Regiment came down & communication trench. The portion of trench held by D Company & E Co. suffered the bringing up of supports to reinforce the front trench. Our supports were greatly handicapped | |

# WAR DIARY or INTELLIGENCE SUMMARY

Army Form C. 2118

(Erase heading not required.)

| Place | Date | Hour | Summary of Events and Information | Remarks and references to Appendices |
|---|---|---|---|---|
| | 1915 May 8 | contd | by this party returning that the point Lt. F.S. PHILLIPS was killed while bringing up the supports. Men of the Cheshire Regiment said the order was to reinforce on the left, but Capt H.T. EDWARDS refused to move as men was killed while holding his trench. Lt. GARBUTT with fixed bayonet hammered at the entrance of the communication trench to hold back men returning. The Germans were by degrees able to bring fire to bear from the rear & the position of the men of the Battn became untenable, eventually almost all were either killed, wounded or captured. Capt. E.C. DIMSDALE (Adjutant) was killed while leading an attack on a machine gun position in a building. The enemy remained the part of B. Co. Supports were seen to be advancing under terrific shell fire. The advance of these supports (afterwards found to be the 12th London Regt) was most gallant, but only a few men survived to reach within 300 yards of the trenches. These men however managed to retire in twos & threes as best they could later with the boys. Their machine gun however was able to get to work from the vicinity of the road in rear of our trenches. The Officer in charge of the gun was soon wounded but Sergt B. HEPBURN fought it until he wounded himself. Mr REID all communication by wire was cut. Col ROBINSON (Comdg Officer) Major WIGHAMS (2nd in Command) came up into the trenches from HdQrs. He may be said here that any artillery reply on our side was totally inadequate to meet the German bombardment. | |

1875 Wt. W593/826 1,000,000 4/15 J.B.C. & A. A.D.S.S./Forms/C.2118.

# WAR DIARY or INTELLIGENCE SUMMARY

Army Form C. 2118

| Place | Date | Hour | Summary of Events and Information | Remarks and references to Appendices |
|---|---|---|---|---|
| | 1915 May 8 (contd) | | Major Williams was killed about 11 a.m. & soon after, Col. Gordon with the Hertfords who were on our left decided to attempt to fall upon new position to cover the flank & prevent any further attempt to fall upon a position in echelon below. This operation was attempted & we proceeded to file into a new line by a communication trench. Col Gordon in Rifle Brigade sending the wounded back. Capt M.C. LLEWELLIN took charge of the left, and party under Lieut EVILL & of the renewing out by the n.g. of communication trench. As they went these trenches only existed for a short distance & they were very narrow & a clear & full of mud & bodies. Casualties were further very heavy as often the ground had to be traversed, which had put us in face of the enemy. There were very few to answer. Eventually the remnant under Capt of rifle machine gun, about 200 who had the support trenches at front of WIELTJE were relieved being shoved by the Royal Irish Regt. The relief of officers left were Major G.A. EVILL, Capt. T.O.M. WILLIAMS, & Lieut G. HEPBURN (wounded). The latter two rejoined the trench (par 2). One later with very heavy casualties. They were forced up by numbers but were fine & also opened a murderous rifle fire on the enemy who tried to get round their flank, they were seen to fall and move round to the trenches adjoining & shot & those that were able to fly. 300 or thereabouts, Col Gordon ordered them to retake & retake duets of Trench trying to get to Bde. & grasp trench at the confluent to refuge. Casualties to regiment were enormous but only did the come in again the trenches were handed over | |
| | | | of the 1st battalion Regt under Lieut MONK was our own night, and | |

# WAR DIARY or INTELLIGENCE SUMMARY

Army Form C. 2118

| Place | Date | Hour | Summary of Events and Information | Remarks and references to Appendices |
|---|---|---|---|---|
| | 1915 May 8 contd | | and though their guns were turned more than once, they stuck to their place, still very good work now as wellas earlier in the day, when they were more advanced position towards evening other regiments came up manned the trenches, those coming to our portion being Dublin Fusiliers. The survivors of our Regiment spent the night in dug-outs about 600 yards behind these trenches. Major Edwill & Capt OM WILLIAMS being at Hd Qrs Dug-out of 1st Welsh Regt. Casualties for May 8th 1915. Officers Killed 5, Wounded 5, Wounded & Prisoner 1 — since died of Wounds, Wounded & Missing 2, Missing 1, Prisoner 1, Total 21. Other Ranks Killed 33, Wounded & Missing 82, Missing 319, Total 434 | |

# WAR DIARY or INTELLIGENCE SUMMARY

Army Form C. 2118

| Place | Date | Hour | Summary of Events and Information | Remarks and references to Appendices |
|---|---|---|---|---|
| | 1915 May 9 | | At midday, Major EVILL & Capt WILLIAMS marched back to the hutting YPRES (near BRIELEN) with 10 men all that remained of the Regiment in the firing line. Their route was one everywhere marked by numerous shell holes & a good number of dead horses & men. This party arrived at about 3.30 p.m at the huts where were parts of LIFE GUARDS & LEICESTERSHIRE Yeomanry. The remaining survivors of May 8th had been collected at our transport at VLAMERTINGE by Lieut. s/ nerving all. These joined up at the huts in the evening. Casualties trench strength of battn on this date – Officers 8 Ranks 129. | |
| | "10. | | Bn marched to own transport fields at VLAMERTINGE at 1 p.m. The 1st Monmouths together with the remnants of the 12th London Regt (Rangers) under the strength of one Company) were warned to move to the trenches under Major EVILL in the evening. The 2 Regiments were paraded for funerals of encouragement spoken by Major EVILL. The Order later cancelled & ordered to move to Huts at YPRES instead of. | |
| | "11. | | Huts YPRES. A Staff Officer (28th Division) came to Huts & interviewed Major EVILL & Capt WILLIAMS to investigate a statement of the Germans claiming to have captured 800 men of Suffolk Regt on May 8th & to inquire if any information with | |

# WAR DIARY
## or
## INTELLIGENCE SUMMARY

Army Form C. 2118

| Place | Date | Hour | Summary of Events and Information | Remarks and references to Appendices |
|---|---|---|---|---|
| | 1915 May 11 cont | | regard to surrender could be given. Major Evill stated that he saw groups of men going forward under heavy rifle fire all along way to the right, but owing to the distance it was impossible for him to identify them. It seems desirable to mention this enquiry in view of the Official report of the action of May 8th. The 1st Monmouths marched to bivouac again to transports at VLAMERTINGHE at 5 p.m. | |
| | "12 | | Marched to Bivouac on POPERINGHE-ABEELE road with 12th London Regt under command of Major Evill. | |
| | "13 | | Rest day. Moved to farm billet on same road. | |
| | "14 | | Moved at 1 p.m. in Motor Omnibuses to HERZEELE arriving 4 p.m. Billeted in 2 farms. [Major Evill went on 5 days leave] LT. A.L. EVANS + LT. S.R. MARTYN | |
| | "15 | | Major EVILL went on 5 days leave reported for duty. | |

# WAR DIARY or INTELLIGENCE SUMMARY.

Army Form C. 2118.

(Erase heading not required.)

| Hour, Date, Place | Summary of Events and Information | Remarks and references to Appendices |
|---|---|---|
| May 16th to 20th 1915 | Still at HERZEELE resting with short route march each day. | |
| May 21st 1915. | At HERZEELE. An Inter-Brigade reviewed the Welsh, Suffolk, Cheshire, Northumbd Fusiliers and 1st Mon. Regt in HERZEELE square at 10am and thanked them for they were in holding the line E of YPRES against the enemy in spite of a bombardment by artillery unprecedented in the history of war and in spite of their enormous numbers and the use of gases. The Commander in Chief congratulates the Regiment. | |
| May 22nd 1915 | Moved composite Brigade including 1 Mon Regt (who had reinforcements starting at 10pm) to BALLOON WOOD FLAMERTINGHE leaving at 6pm. Interior echelon went into bivouac [Cheshire Regt + Suffolk Regt following. Distance between columns 1 mile.] Halt in POPERINGHE. No men fell out. 3rd Battalion Mon Regt came into bivouac on west side of major BRIDGE. | |
| May 24th 1915 | Order to move under Major Bridge to HUTS YPRES reed at 3am. Reconnoitred route across country under cover to HUTS YPRES. Journey to HUTS at 11am further to move from there to G.H.Q. line Army H.Q. received at 10 [?] Moved out in column following Welsh Regt. Suffolk Regt via Canal bridge S of YPRES. Heavy shelling before entering Armed Q.H.Q line. E of ZILLEBEKE LAKE at 4.30pm. Occupied trenches | |

Army Form C. 2118.

# WAR DIARY
## or
## INTELLIGENCE SUMMARY.
*(Erase heading not required.)*

| Hour, Date, Place | Summary of Events and Information | Remarks and references to Appendices |
|---|---|---|
| May 25th 1915 | Orders to move to Brig HQ received at 1 am. Heavy fire from machine guns. Occupied trenches R of MENIN ROAD - attacked by 84 and 80 Brigade on German trenches unsuccessful. [Very heavy casualties in WELSH.] Casualties 3 Officers wounded & Bn relieved at 230 pm by 8th Brigade. [Carried tools along Railway Embankment to Company at LILLEGATE.] Marched to BALLOON WOOD FLAMERTINGHE. Arrived at 2/30 am | |
| May 26th 1915 | Rested. | |
| May 27th 1915 | 2nd Battalion Mon Regt came into Bivouac | |
| May 28th 1915 | Moved from BALLOON WOOD to HERZEELE as a composite battalion under command of Major BRIDGE - arrived 6 pm went into billets. | |
| May 29th 1915 | Composite Battalion Paraded for Inspection by G.O.C. V Army - General Allenby in HERZEELE Square. | |
| May 30th 1915 | Organization of composite battalion proceeded with. Addressed Units by General BOLS who said that the present arrangement were temporary and that each Battalion would be reformed when sufficient numbers were found in the Recent Battalion. Battalion paraded at 6 pm & reorganised all A B C & D Companies were knitted together an order to keep within together at stood required of Capt Rickts 2nd mon regt | |
| May 31st 1915 | Organization of Companies | |

The MONMOUTHSHIRE Regiment.

(1. 2. 3. 1st Amalgamated)

Army Form C. 2118.

# WAR DIARY
## or
## INTELLIGENCE SUMMARY.
(Erase heading not required.)

Instructions regarding War Diaries and Intelligence Summaries are contained in F.S. Regs., Part II. and the Staff Manual respectively. Title pages will be prepared in manuscript.

| Hour, Date, Place | Summary of Events and Information | Remarks and references to Appendices |
|---|---|---|
| 28 May 1915. HERZEELE | Whole command of Major Pawlge (3rd Br Mon Regt) The three Monmouthshire Battalions amalgamated and ordained by the Brigadier (General Bols) who said the amalgamated battalions were paraded eventually returned. Organisation of companies proceeded with all "A" Companies of each battalion + B C & D respectively being joined together. Battalion reviewed 16 Companies | Amalgamation Strengths o/rs. O.R. 1st Battn.  11 - 218 (Major Ewill) 2nd Battn. 19 - 580 (Capt. SPARKES) 3rd Battn. 11 - 250 (Major BRIDGE) — 41 - 1048 |
| 29 May | do | Organising and equipping. Musketry on Short Range. Brigade parade in HERZEELE Square for King's Birthday under Major TOKE Welsh Regiment. Following officers joined Captain E. Edwards Lieut Gates & H Davies (2nd Mon) and Lieut Raines (1st B). |  |
| 30 May | do | Battalion Parade and Musketry. Lieuts Gates and Davis returned to Base |  |
| 31 May | do | Battalion and Company Parades. Musketry |  |

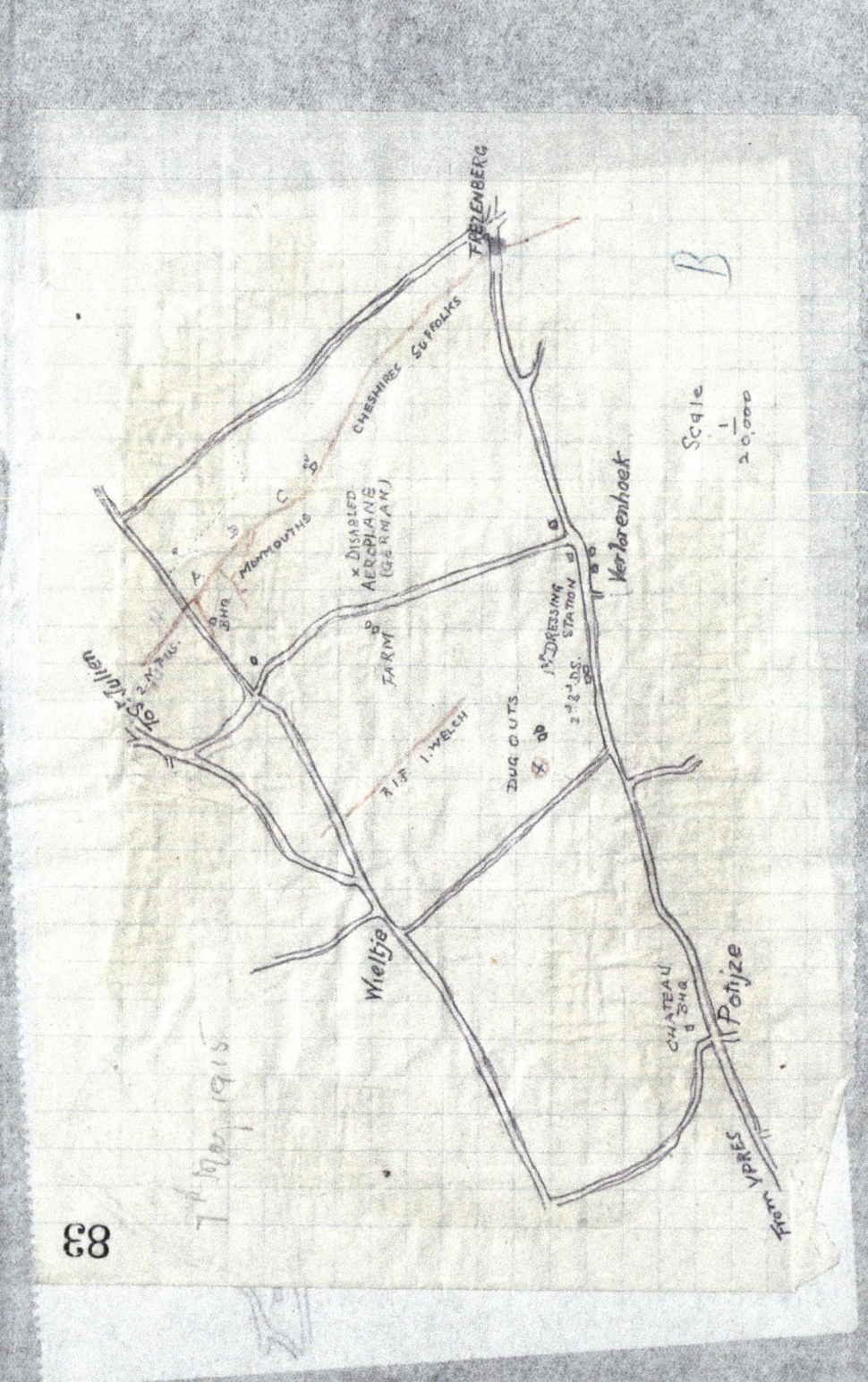

28th Division.
84th Brigade.

# WAR DIARY

Amalgamated Battalion of 1st, 2nd & 3rd

## MONMOUTHSHIRES

JUNE 1915

Army Form C. 2118.

# WAR DIARY
or
## INTELLIGENCE SUMMARY.
(Erase heading not required.)

Instructions regarding War Diaries and Intelligence Summaries are contained in F. S. Regs., Part II. and the Staff Manual respectively. Title pages will be prepared in manuscript.

| Place | Date | Hour | Summary of Events and Information | Remarks and references to Appendices |
|---|---|---|---|---|
| HERZEELE | 1 June | | Battalion & company parade - musketry | |
| | 2 June | do | Lieut. A.C. Sole and 2 Lieut. North went on leave | |
| | 3 June | do | ditto | |
| | 4 June | do | ditto | |
| | 5 June | do | ditto | |
| | 6 June | do | Captain Hon. Maj: Pennymore Lieut D.M. A Foy + 2 Lieut Crossley + Bridge went on leave | |
| | 7 June | do | ditto | |
| | 8 June | do | ditto | |
| SPA | 9 June | do | Captain Rolls joined as Adjutant vice Capt. V.B. Ramsden | |
| | 10 June | do | Ordrs to move tomorrow received | |
| | 11 June | do | Brigade moved to ROSENHILBEK · RENINGHELST · na WATOU · POPERINGHE Suffolk Reg.t Transport blocked road near WATOU · delayed column for ¾ hour arrived at 8 P.M. Distance about 10 miles. No men fell out Strength 30 officers 999 other ranks | MOVE. |

(73989) W4141—463. 400,000. 9/14. H.&J.Ltd. Forms/C. 2118/10.

The MONMOUTHSHIRE REGIMENT.

(1,2,3 rd Batt~ Amalgamated)

Army Form C. 2118.

# WAR DIARY
## or
## INTELLIGENCE SUMMARY.
*(Erase heading not required.)*

Instructions regarding War Diaries and Intelligence Summaries are contained in F.S. Regs., Part II. and the Staff Manual respectively. Title pages will be prepared in manuscript.

| Hour, Date, Place | | | Summary of Events and Information | Remarks and references to Appendices |
|---|---|---|---|---|
| 1915 June | | | | |
| 12 | ROSENHILBEK RENINGHELST. | | Moved to DICKEBUSCH – Marched at 6 p.m. and relieved 1/16 K.R.R. in trenches M2. 15. O. 2. | MOVE |
| 13th | VIERSTRAAT | | Relief completed 2 a.m. Batt. H.Q. GORDON FARM. Casualties 4 wounded – Lieut. J. M. Fry & Lieut Cowley & Bridge returned from leave | Trench duty |
| 14th | — | do | Enemy quiet. A good deal of work to be done in the and communicating trenches which men proceeded with. Casualties 3 wounded | |
| 15th | — | do | Enemy quiet. working parties improving trenches – casualties 3 wounded | |
| 16th | — | do. | Some sniper fire in M1 & M2. Casualties 1 killed 5 wounded. Weather very hot and fine | |
| 17th | — | do | Enemy quiet. casualties 1 Killed 1 wounded | |
| 18th | — | do | Shelling heavy on right of section. Casualties 5 killed 16 wounded. | |
| 19th | — | do | Some shelling but no casualties. | |
| 20th | — | do | Battalion relieved by 1 Welsh and Cheshire Regt. Relief complete without casualty at 1 p.m. C & D Cos to RIDGEWOOD. A + B to PIONEER FARM (B.H.Q.) Total Casualties 7 killed 32 wounded | Relief |
| | | | Brigade Reserve. working parties at night. Bois CARRÉ communication trench & shell trench in rear of P. Trenches which was shelled – 1 killed 5 wounded | |
| 21st | — | do | Present parties – no casualties | |
| 22nd | — | do | do – no casualties | |
| 23rd | — | do | A + B Companies moved to RIDGEWOOD at 7 a.m. B.H.Q. & GORDON FARM. 120 men B.Co. to GORDON FARM | |
| 24th | — | do | Digging fatigue D.Co. completing Bois CARRÉ C.T. 100 men under R.E. 1 killed | |
| 25th | — | do | Digging fatigue – no casualties. 2 Lieut Cayley to hospital | |
| 26th | — | do | Relieved Cheshire Regt. in M1.2.3.M4 SR.W.R. E.R.(BOIS CARRÉ) and Welsh Regt. in N1. N2. N3. N4. N5. N7. N.8. with 3 Cos A + B + D. C Co to RIDGEWOOD. Relief complete at midnight. B.H.Q. in DO. 100's of BRASSERIE – No casualties | Trench duty |
| 27th | — | do | Enemy quiet. Bois CARRÉ shelled and trenches – no casualties – C.T.s w.r.k. carried out of work – Stout trench between N7 and N8 proceeded with. Lieut Cayley & Brain returned from hospital | |

THE MONMOUTHSHIRE REGIMENT.
(1, 2, & 3rd Batt. Amalgamated)

Army Form C. 2118.

WAR DIARY
or
INTELLIGENCE SUMMARY.
(Erase heading not required.)

| Hour, Date, Place | Summary of Events and Information | Remarks and references to Appendices |
|---|---|---|
| 1915<br>28 June VIERSTRAAT. | Enemy quiet - Shell trenches, dug and C.T.s drained - C.T. from N-7<br>to BOISCARRE progressed - casualties 1 wounded. Strength 29 officers 939 o.r.<br>E.B. obtained A Company. Heavy rain & 6mm Lieut Whitehead wounded accidentally by<br>premature burst of rifle grenade - admitted to hospital. | |
| 29 June do | Enemy quiet. | |
| 30 June do | Enemy quiet. Artillery bombardment of SICKEBUSCH.<br>The following names appeared in the Honors and Distinctions Gazette<br>Lt. Col. H. Worsley-Gough C.M.G. 3rd Batt. Mon Regt.<br>Captain A.H. Edwards Military Cross 2nd Batt.<br>Captain A.J.H. Bowen D.S.O 2nd Batt.<br>Major W.A. Lewis 3rd Batt. ⎫<br>Capt: R.F.D. Gattie do ⎬ Mentioned in despatches<br>Lt. R.B. Conoly 2 Batt. ⎭<br>69 Co Serjt Major J. Gill 3rd Batt.<br>S.M.3 a/c S.M. Medlop G.S.<br>6038<br>2058 Serjt. C. Lore D.C.M. 2nd Batt.<br>1608 Pte Hemmings W. D.C.M. | Mobilise "May"<br>Comdg the Monmouthshire Regt<br>30 June 1915 |

Copy.

# WAR DIARY.

## 1915
## JULY.

**1915**
**July**

| | |
|---|---|
| 1st | Battalion still in trenches |
| 2nd | - do - |
| 3rd | Battalion relieved by Welch Regiment A, C and D. Coys. in Ridge Wood B Coy. from Ridge Wood to Gordon Farm. Hqrs. Gordon Farm. Relief completed 12 midnight without casualties. |
| 4th | Dickebusch. Battalion moved to billets in rear Bde. Hqrs. at 8 p.m. |
| 5th | Representatives of three battalions interviewed by General Bols as to separation. Battalion moved to Canada Huts at 8 p.m. |
| 6th | Companies washed and musketry. |
| 7th | Working parties of 150 men by night on communication trenches. 2 casualties. Parade for inspection by General Bulfin. |
| 8th | Working parties of 650 men on subsidiary line and communication trench to M 2. No casualties. |
| 9th | Sports: very successful. |
| 10th | Relieved 1/Welch Regiment from M 2 to N 5 completed at midnight. No casualties. Captain Gattie appointed Adjutant. |
| 11th | Quiet day. Trenches had not been left in a clean condition. |
| 12th | Enemy quiet. Some shelling. Enemy mine reported under N.3 Engineers warned and inspected it. |
| 13th | Quiet day. Col. Pritchard 10/Gloster Regt. was conducted round the trenches on an instructional tour. Orders received for relief tomorrow night by 9th Brigade. |
| 14th | Relieved by 4th Battalion Royal Fusiliers. Very wet. Relief completed 4 a.m. No casualties. Marched to Canada Huts for night. |
| 15th | Marched to Westoutre at 8 p.m. Billeted in Farm House west of town. Two companies in field. |
| 16th | Major Bridge and Os C. Coys. to Kemmel to reconnoitre trenches E 2 to H 4 Battalion moved to Badajoz Huts, Locre, arriving at 8.50 p.m. Huts were claimed by Yorkshire Regt. but having been allotted by Staff Captain 84th Brigade, were retained by Battalion. |

1915
July

17th    Locre. Inspection of kits.

18th    Church parade. Reconnoitring trenches.

19th    March to Kemmel. Relieved Welch Regt. in E 2 to F 6. 1 coy 6/Welch T.F. attached for instruction. Relief completed 11.13 p.m. No casualties.

20th    Kemmel - Enemy quiet. Fire at Lindenhoek cross roads. Few shells followed. No casualties. Order for 2/Monmouthshire Regt; to separate.

21st    Quiet day. Few shells fell by Battn. Hqrs. No casualties.

22nd    Enemy quiet. Some shelling near Hqrs. Orders for 2nd Battn. to proceed to join 12th Infantry Brigade and for battalion to be relieved by 1/Welch Regt. Battalion relieved by Welch Regt. Relief completed by 12 midnight.

23rd    Locre. Battalion paraded and 1st, 2nd and 3rd Battalions separately paraded. 1st Batt. 1 coy, 2nd Batt. 2 Coys, and 3rd Battn. 1 coy.

24th    2nd Battan. Monmouthshire Regt. paraded at 12.30 p.m. and left to join the 12th Infantry Brigade under command of Capt. E. Edwards:

    Strength 1st Battn. 7 officers, 193 other ranks.
            2nd Battn. 12 " 476 "
            3rd 8 " 273 "

25th    Church parade. Battalion formed in to two coys.

    No. 1 Coy. 1/Monmouth Regt.
    No. 2 Coy. 3/ do.

under command of Lieut.-Colonel W.S. Bridge. Digging fatigues two parties 220 men. Vierstraat switch and carrying party to Suffolk Regt.

26th    Organization of Coys. into Platoons for instruction of Specialists:

    No. 1 Platoon    Machine Gunners;
    "   2    "       Bombers
    "   3    "       Signallers
    "   4    "       Details.

Orders received that battalion would relieve Welch Regt. on night 28th/29th. Draft of 75 men arrived for 3rd Battn. together with the following officers:

    Capts. H.G. Tyler    W.W. Wilson;
    Lieuts. H.A. Hodges, J.O. Carpenter, B.L. Jones, M.A. Sefton.
    2/Lieuts. J.A. Findlay, A.G.I.A. Goddard, H.C. Williams

Officers for 1st Battalion, Lieut. R.C.L. Thomas, 2/Lieuts. H.J. Ballinger, C. Kirby, E.A. Tisdall, and L.H.C. Smith.

28th    Organization into platoons for instruction abandoned and Coys. reorganized for trench duty. No. 1 Coy. with following officers attached Lts. R.C.C. Thomas, A.L. Evans, J.F.C. Raikes, 2/Lts. W.E.C.A. Darby, H.J. Ballinger, C. Kirby, E.G. Tisdall and L.H.C. Smith.

    No. 2 Coy. Capt. H.G. Tyler, Lt. H.A. Hodges, J.O. Carpenter; 2/Lieut. J.A. Findlay and 2/Lt. A G I A Goddard.

1915

July
27th
28th (contd.)   No. 3 Coy. Capt. O.W.D. Steele and W.W. Wilson, Lts.
L.W. Martyn, B.L. Jones, 2/Lt. H.C. Williams

28th   Coys. washed. Inspection of kit, respirators sprayed etc. Battalion paraded at 7.30 p.m. for trench duty. Relieved 1st and 6th Welch Regt. in F.2, F.4, F.6, SP 8 SP 8 and Regent Street. Dugouts. Relief completed midnight Strength officers, 26, other ranks, 405.

29th   Kemmel. Fairly heavy shelling. Our artillery shelled Wytschaele and in reply enemy shelled Kemmel heavily. Two casualties.

30th   Enemy very busy on work at Spanbroekmolen by night. Rapid fire opened on them from F.4, but they continued to work. Artillery then fired on them. Heavy shell fire on F 6. Parapet broken in two places. Two casualties.

31st   Enemy again busy on working parties. Wire in front of F 2 repaired and reconnaissance of enemy position carried out by Lieut. A.L. Evans.

Copy.

# WAR DIARY.

## 1915
## JULY.

1915
July

| | |
|---|---|
| 1st | Battalion still in trenches |
| 2nd | - do - |
| 3rd | Battalion relieved by Welch Regiment A, C and D. Coys. in Ridge Wood B Coy. from Ridge Wood to Gordon Farm. Hqrs. Gordon Farm. Relief completed 12 midnight without casualties. |
| 4th | Dickebusch. Battalion moved to billets in rear Bde. Hqrs. at 8 p.m. |
| 5th | Representatives of three battalions interviewed by General Bols as to separation. Battalion moved to Canada Huts at 8 p.m. |
| 6th | Companies washed and musketry. |
| 7th | Working parties of 150 men by night on communication trenches. 2 casualties. Parade for inspection by General Bulfin. |
| 8th | Working parties of 650 men on subsidiary line and communication trench to M 2. No casualties. |
| 9th | Sports: very successful. |
| 10th | Relieved 1/Welch Regiment from M 2 to N 5 completed at midnight. No casualties. Captain Gattie appointed Adjutant. |
| 11th | Quiet day. Trenches had not been left in a clean condition. |
| 12th | Enemy quiet. Some shelling. Enemy mine reported under N.3 Engineers warned and inspected it. |
| 13th | Quiet day. Col. Pritchard 10/Gloster Regt. was conducted round the trenches on an instructional tour. Orders received for relief tomorrow night by 9th Brigade. |
| 14th | Relieved by 4th Battalion Royal Fusiliers. Very wet. Relief completed 4 a.m. No casualties. Marched to Canada Huts for night. |
| 15th | Marched to Westoutre at 8 p.m. Billeted in Farm House west of town. Two companies in field. |
| 16th | Major Bridge and Os C. Coys. to Kemmel to reconnoitre trenches E 2 to H 4 Battalion moved to Badajoz Huts, Locre, arriving at 8.50 p.m. Huts were claimed by Yorkshire Regt. but having been allotted by Staff Captain 84th Brigade, were retained by Battalion. |

1915

July

17th        Locre. Inspection of kits.

18th        Church parade. Reconnoitring trenches.

19th        March to Kemmel. Relieved Welch Regt. in E 2 to F 6. 1 coy 6/Welch T.F. attached for instruction. Relief completed 11.13 p.m. No casualties.

20th        Kemmel - Enemy quiet. Fire at Lindenhoek cross roads. Few shells followed. No casualties. Order for 2/Monmouthshire Regt. to separate.

21st        Quiet day. Few shells fell by Battn. Hqrs. No casualties.

22nd        Enemy quiet. Some shelling near Hqrs. Orders for 2nd Battn. to proceed to join 12th Infantry Brigade and for battalion to be relieved by 1/Welch Regt. Battalion relieved by Welch Regt. Relief completed by 12 midnight.

23rd        Locre. Battalion paraded and 1st, 2nd and 3rd Battalions separately paraded. 1st Batt. 1 coy, 2nd Batt. 2 Coys, and 3rd Battn. 1 coy.

24th        2nd Battan. Monmouthshire Regt. paraded at 12.30 p.m. and left to join the 12th Infantry Brigade under command of Capt. E. Edwards:

        Strength 1st Battn. 7 officers, 193 other ranks.
                2nd Battn. 12 " 476 "
                3rd         8 " 273 "

25th        Church parade. Battalion formed in to two coys.

        No. 1 Coy. 1/Monmouth Regt.
        No. 2 Coy. 3/   do.

under command of Lieut.-Colonel W.S. Bridge. Digging fatigues two parties 220 men. Vierstraat switch and carrying party to Suffolk Regt.

26th        Organization of Coys. into Platoons for instruction of Specialists:

        No. 1 Platoon    Machine Gunners;
        "   2    "         Bombers
        "   3    "         Signallers
        "   4    "         Details.

Orders received that battalion would relieve Welch Regt. on night 28th/29th. Draft of 75 men arrived for 3rd Battn. together with the following officers:

        Capts. H.G. Tyler    W.W. Wilson;
        Lieuts. H.A. Hodges, J.O. Carpenter, B.L. Jones, M.A. Sefton.
        2/Lieuts. J.A. Findlay, A.G.I.A. Goddard, H.C. Williams

Officers for 1st Battalion, Lieut. R.C.L. Thomas, 2/Lieuts. H.J. Ballinger, C. Kirby, E.A. Tisdall, and L.H.C. Smith.

27th        Organization into platoons for instruction abandoned and Coys. reorganized for trench duty. No. 1 Coy. with following officers attached Lts. R.C.C. Thomas, A.L. Evans, J.F.C. Raikes, 2/Lts. W.E.C.A. Darby, H.J. Ballinger, C. Kirby, E.G. Tisdall and L.H.C. Smith.

    No. 2 Coy. Capt. H.G. Tyler, Lt. H.A. Hodges, J.O. Carpenter; 2/Lieut. J.A. Findlay and 2/Lt. A G I A Goddard.

1915

July

27th
28th (contd.) No. 3 Coy. Capt. O.W.D.Steele and W.W. Wilson, Lts. L.W. Martyn, B.L. Jones, 2/Lt. H.C. Williams

28th  Coys. washed. Inspection of kit, respirators sprayed etc. Battalion paraded at 7.30 p.m. for trench duty. Relieved 1st and 6th Welch Regt. in F.2, F.4, F.6, SP 8 SP 8 and Regent Street. Dugouts. Relief completed midnight Strength officers, 26, other ranks, 405.

29th  Kemmel. Fairly heavy shelling. Our artillery shelled Wytschaele and in reply enemy shelled Kemmel heavily. Two casualties.

30th  Enemy very busy on work at Spanbroekmolen by night. Rapid fire opened on them from F.4, but they continued to work. Artillery then fired on them. Heavy shell fire on F 6. Parapet broken in two places. Two casualties.

31st  Enemy again busy on working parties. Wire in front of F 2 repaired and reconnaissance of enemy position carried out by Lieut. A.L. Evans.

28th Division
84th Brigade

# WAR DIARY

Amalgamated Battalion of 1st & 3rd

## MONMOUTHSHIRES

## AUGUST 1915

Battalions resumed independant formation on
August 11th 1915. 3rd Mons. joined 83rd Bde.

**Army Form C. 2118.**

# WAR DIARY
## or
## INTELLIGENCE SUMMARY.
*(Erase heading not required.)*

Instructions regarding War Diaries and Intelligence Summaries are contained in F.S. Regs., Part II. and the Staff Manual respectively. Title pages will be prepared in manuscript.

| Hour, Date, Place | Summary of Events and Information | Remarks and references to Appendices |
|---|---|---|
| 1915 LINDENHOEK 1st August | Enemy quiet. A mine exploded in G.I. which caught the German mine which had reached our parapet. Squeals and shouts were heard from minewound. Lieut. Conley was responsible for the successful countermining which probably saved the trench G.I. loss by the Northumberland Fusiliers - Some Coal Box on but no Casualties. The garrison of the line is reinforced and at night the men are on an hour and off an hour and at dawn including officers sentries and sanitary police & doing sentry - Captain G.W.D. Steel Sick - Gason resumes for night 2/3. 2 Lieut. C.A. Vickers & N.T. Llewellin joined battalion. | |
| 2nd August | Quiet night - Captain W. Wilson was shot through the head while looking over the parapet and killed instantly. 2nd Lieut. C.T. Vachell and N.T.C. Llewellin joined the Battalion. Battalion relieved by 6th Welch Regiment commanded by Lt. Col. and Surian Crockr. Stewart. Relief completed 1.30 am. Marched to LOCRE. | |
| 3rd August 4th August | Battalion in BADAJOS HUTS. LOCRE. Battalion moved to KEMMEL SHELTERS LOCRE on from 1st Suffolk Regt. 1 company for working party attached to 6th Welch Regt. | |
| 5th August | Battalion still in Kemmel Shelters. Capt. D. M. Williams Lieut. & T. Crawford rejoined the battalion from S.R. Marsh not Hospital doing. Mr went still remained in England. 5th August. | |

Army Form C. 2118.

# WAR DIARY
## or
## INTELLIGENCE SUMMARY.
(Erase heading not required.)

| Hour, Date, Place | Summary of Events and Information | Remarks and references to Appendices |
|---|---|---|
| August 6th 1915 | Battalion still in KEMMEL SHELTERS. Draft arrived for Batt. composed of 1 Lieut., [illegible] — 1st L.N. Lancs., 2nd Lieut Drennan 11th Rifle Brigade and 23 other ranks. | |
| | 8pm  do  Lt Col Hoppe 27th Battery 24th Bde R.F.A. reported and took over at LOCRE 157 O.R. ranks Batt relieved by 2nd[?] Kings Royal Rifles R.B. in LOCRE Huts [illegible] Cmd [illegible] | |
| August 7th 1915 | Battalion still [illegible] the [illegible] Hello to 2nd Cheshire Regt. H.Q. [illegible] into the huts [illegible] | |
| August 8th 1915 | Church parades for all denominations except R.C.s. the drafts of the 1st & 3rd were bathed. | |
| August 9th 1915 | General reorganisation to prepare for the transfer of the 3rd Normandie hills 85th Brigade. Billets heavily shelled by English order. At the regimental Staff in LOCRE the reorganisation being carried by a Brigade of Kitchener's Army being brought into the District. A Academy of Mrs Thompson's musketry programme received. 6 Cat on S.B.B.? S.B.J. different on two types the [illegible] Ever being taken outs, 2 left with the 6th field. | |

# WAR DIARY
## or
## INTELLIGENCE SUMMARY.
*(Erase heading not required.)*

Army Form C. 2118.

| Hour, Date, Place | Summary of Events and Information | Remarks and references to Appendices |
|---|---|---|
| 11th August 1916. | Paraded at 5.30 am to reorganise (Platoons) for tench duty and again at 11 am. Lt Bagley attended the parade to visit the battalion generally. The Commanding Officer and Bry General B.G. in also present to inspect the battalion. At 6 pm Regtl HQrs rejoined Bn & marched W of HQrs 83rd Brigade. Bttn battalion again relieved the Cheshires in front line trenches. Major Evill returned from leave and assumed command of 11/2nd Bn. Relief commenced at 7.30 pm & carried out without taking over trenches. RE F2, F6, F2a & F4. Relief completed by 12 midnight without casualty. Dispositions of Coys same as attached map. Report to Bgde - 0.6 Left/Coeuli interior walls all trenches during night. | |
| 12 August LINDENHOEK. | Quiet day. Major Sell visited all trenches in morning. Left and relieved visited all trenches in evening. Lieut K.C. Railey & 2/Lt Roberts (attached No.1 Coy for instructing R.P.) reported for duty in the afternoon. Casualties: 1 Drummer Regt. dd. 1 NCO 2 wounded during nightwork. | |

Army Form C. 2118.

# WAR DIARY
## or
## INTELLIGENCE SUMMARY.
*(Erase heading not required.)*

Instructions regarding War Diaries and Intelligence Summaries are contained in F.S. Regs., Part II. and the Staff Manual respectively. Title pages will be prepared in manuscript.

| Hour, Date, Place | Summary of Events and Information | Remarks and references to Appendices |
|---|---|---|
| 1915 August 16th LOCRE | Billet LOCRE. Re-organisation into 4 nucleus companies | |
| Aug. 17 LOCRE | Parade. Physical Training & Inspection. Officers posted to companies. A draft of 25 other Ranks reported from the Base. The Battn. employed on Digging & camping fatigues at night to KEMMEL trenches. LOCRE hospital & Officers Rest Station. MONT NOIR. Hospital. Sickroom LOCRE still busy. Digging & Camping fatigues at | |
| Aug 18th LOCRE | night at KEMMEZ. Parade. Close order Drill. Digging fatigue morning (20 men). | |
| Aug 19th & LOCRE | Small party Digging fatigue in morning Currently 45th Field Ambulance — very successful. | |
| Aug 20st LOCRE | A permanent working party of 2 NCOs & one Batman for motor the Commander in Chief VIA the GHELLIA billeted in ARCADIA HUTS DOTS | |
| | Lieut R.C.L. THOMAS has been acting Adjutant since 11th August. | Owen |

Army Form C. 2118.

# WAR DIARY
## or
## INTELLIGENCE SUMMARY.
(Erase heading not required.)

| Hour, Date, Place | Summary of Events and Information | Remarks and references to Appendices |
|---|---|---|
| 1915<br>August 13th<br>LINDENHOEK | A quiet morning. A good bit of shelling over our trenches & of the night with very heavy cold [?] fire stuff. 5.30 to 7.30 pm Capt R.C. Raikes + 2/Lt Roberts went to trenches F6 + F2 for instruction. Major Ebb sick - went to Field Ambulance. Approximately nothing in Command. KEMMEL shelled in afternoon. 3 Officers Yorkshire Dragoons attached with piquet to our trenches for instruction. Returned 10 am. New Communication trench between F6 + F2 proceeded with. Casualties nil. | |
| Aug 14th<br>LINDENHOEK | Quiet day. One platoon in F2 relieved by one platoon F6. Lieut Sir Martin reported for duty from Hospital. New Communication trench F6 & F2 proceeded with. Casualties nil. | |
| Aug 15. LINDENHOEK | Quiet morning. Attend [?] Battle Headqrs. 3.15 pm. An artillery Spie [?] C short retaliation expected. Very little shelling in either side toward Situation resumed at 5 pm. Relieved by Cornwall Regt. Returned to old billet LOCRE Casualties nil. | (sgn) |

# WAR DIARY
## or
## INTELLIGENCE SUMMARY.
(Erase heading not required.)

Army Form C. 2118.

Instructions regarding War Diaries and Intelligence Summaries are contained in F.S. Regs., Part II. and the Staff Manual respectively. Title pages will be prepared in manuscript.

| Hour, Date, Place | Summary of Events and Information | Remarks and references to Appendices |
|---|---|---|
| 1915 Aug 21st LOCRE | Major C.A. BILL returned to E. duty from MONT NOIR. Officers registration & Lists see annexed. | |
| Aug 22nd LOCRE | Church Parades. B & D Companies took over S.P.8 & S.P.9 2/Lt JORDAN-LLOYD took up 2 machine guns. | |
| Aug 23rd LOCRE | 2/Lt PHILLIPS, 2/Lt James Empire Bunny Section dated 25/8/15. The C.O. & Capt. WILLIAMS visited the companies in S.P.8 & S.P.9. Lt WIGSON FIELD 4 + a draft of 107 reported for duty from 2nd line. | |
| Aug 24th LOCRE | A & C Companies doing work on the VIERSTRAAT line. C.O. inspected the breastworks. Draft strength was 5 - Officers 24 O.Rs. Ranks. | |
| Aug 25 LOCRE | C Company # to duty in VIERSTRAAT line. Following officers reported for duty 2/Lt LEWIS A.G.) from 3rd Battn. 2/Lt PEEL H.L.) Sentembre Bordeaux | |

Army Form C. 2118.

# WAR DIARY
## or
## INTELLIGENCE SUMMARY.
(Erase heading not required.)

Instructions regarding War Diaries and Intelligence Summaries are contained in F.S. Regs., Part II. and the Staff Manual respectively. Title pages will be prepared in manuscript.

| Hour, Date, Place | Summary of Events and Information | Remarks and references to Appendices |
|---|---|---|
| 1915 | | |
| August 27th LOCRE | A Company took over S.P.8 & S.P.9 overnight. Other Companies Company + Batn. drill. Physical training. 2/Lt DAVIDSON. C. reported for duty from 3rd Bn. S.Wales Borderers. Capt. & A/C HEPBURN attached 172nd Co. R.E. awarded D.S.O. Riflemen ? ... D.C.M. | |
| " 28th LOCRE | Company Tactical + Physical opening Elliotree MARCEAU vacated Battn. as Interpreter. Battn. + route marching by Companies. | |
| " 29th LOCRE | Day Inspn. of 4 Officers & two O.R. in VIERSTRAAT Line Church Parades small in consequence. | |
| " 30th LOCRE | Fatigue party in same line. Other Strengths as yesterday. | |
| " 31st LOCRE | C.O's inspection of Battn. Some shelling in vicinity of S.P.8 & S.P.9 casualties. 1 man wounded. The total strength of Battn. on this date including all Detached Officers O.R. is -- Officers 27. O.Ranks 1412. | |

(73989) W4141—463. 400,000. 9/14. H.&J.Ltd. Forms/C. 2118/10.

Over.

woasl stieg/YYY